OWEN BRYAN JR.

I0142752

OBSERVATION
OF THE
MOMENT

ANALYZING MOMENTS IN EVERYDAY LIFE
THROUGH **POETRY**

Every effort has been made to trace or contact all copyright holders.

Copyright © 2020 by Owen A. Bryan, Jr.

All rights reserved. No part of this book may be reproduced or used in any manner without written permission of the copyright owner except for the use of quotations in a book review. For more information, address: info@owenbryanjr.com

First Edition January 2020
Revised Edition March 2021

Cover designed by 100Covers.com
Interior designed by FormattedBooks.com

ISBN 978-1-7345432-3-0 (paperback)
ISBN 978-1-7345432-1-6 (e-book)

Published by Owen A. Bryan Jr.
www.owenbryanjr.com
Twitter: @owenbryanjr1
Instagram: @owenbryanjr
Facebook: @owenbryanjr
Tumblr: @owenbryanjr

TABLE OF CONTENTS

ACKNOWLEDGMENTS

THIS DEBUT BOOK of poetry captures my life experiences to date, including how I've been touched by numerous people with whom I've associated. You all have played a part in my crafting this work.

From family members, to organizations (Collegiate 100 of Armstrong Atlantic, NSBE UCF, Toastmasters, LTD) that I am thankful to have been a part of, to co-workers (JCB Construction and Jordan Brothers Construction) I had the pleasure to work, I've learned a lot from you. You have helped me become who I am today.

Special thanks to my co-worker, Joyce Cajarop, at Jordan Brothers Construction. Her enthusiastic support of my work was instrumental in my getting this book out. Joyce describes my poetry as "motivational speaking in written form." She has stated on multiple occasions her strong conviction that for the many people out there who are down and out my poetry could help them move through their tough times.

Owen Bryan Jr.
January 2020

INTRODUCTION

THE HOW AND WHY OF
OBSERVATION OF THE MOMENT

The first meaning of *Observation of the Moment* is that the majority of my poems were written from memories of the past. Some of these poems I wrote years after the events they are about, and other poems I wrote the very day the events occurred. I reflected on memories in life and analyzed my thoughts and behavior reacting to those moments.

The second meaning of the title refers to how I composed my poems in moments of remembrance—in a way, capturing my thoughts on paper during these reflections.

This book was composed organically, meaning I never planned on writing it. The combination of enjoying the writing process, and the positive feedback I received from acquaintances and people I did not know, led to my focusing on issues that I could express through poetry. After I'd written and compiled a number of poems, the possibility of a book emerged. As I wrote more poetry, I began crafting motivational messages to coincide with my poetry. With my poetry, I found it to be a vehicle that I can show other people my reality in a way that can help lead positive changes in their lives.

Now, I am not a licensed therapist, nor have I taken any psychology courses. And I am definitely not a miracle worker. But I have gained knowledge from improving myself and life situations, and I believe I can help others experiencing similar circumstances.

My email contact is info@owenbryanjr.com. I welcome any comments, feedback, questions, or concerns you may have after reading my book.

POEMS

It's Tough Love

As a kid,
I remember
Growing up in New York
At the end of the school day in elementary—
The ice cream truck would be parked at the end of the street.
Each day laughing, kicking it,
And sharing stories with friends.

One afternoon my dad was parked,
Waiting to pick me up near the truck.
I saw my friend asking kids around,
"Hey, I can borrow a dolla?".
I followed suit
Not thinking anything was wrong.

When I came back to see my dad
With a blanketed look of disbelief
Staring at me,
(I'm looking back like "What did I do?!?!"),
That very moment he scolded me—

**"Neva beg anyone fi a dolla.
If yu need money,
Mus ask mi or yuh mutha"**

Back in my high school days in metro Atlanta,
I was going through a string of—
In-school suspensions, after school detentions,
When one day after school
Called my mom to pick me up
From detention,
(Mind you, home was about 2.5 miles away from school),
I expressed to her the situation,
And she showed no remorse

Retorting back candidly,

"Yuh gonna have to make that walk"

Now,
Psychologists will say
Our childhoods
Told through the lens of the beholder
Can be overly sensationalized,
Exaggerated, taken out of context.
That instance, that period, that time
Becomes one of melancholy and vitriol
As told through the perspective of whom it happened to.

But you and I
Can also see everything as something to learn a lesson from.
Realignment, rewiring of the mind, body and soul,
A sense of growth that was needed
To make you see your life is something you can control.

Reflecting back,
It can be a moment to smile and look at in bliss.

Reborn

God fearing, Higher Power bending,
Walking, locked in, step-by-step,
Entering the valley of the shadow of death.
In this journey, I find myself
Stumbling into the crevices of hopelessness—
My mind jaded, drifting into an abyss,
I ponder on the brevity of life.

I look up… And I speak to God:
"Looking at my world, it seems all I know is losing.
Will I win one time?
The feeling of winning is foreign to me."

I hear no answer.
But I continue pushing onward,
I keep persevering—
Seeing no end in sight,
I begin to dig… And I keep digging…
                    And digging…
                              And digging…
        Until I get to this point
                                        rise
                        to
                begin
            I

From this soulless pit, I dig
A new life, a new me
Coming through the dirt,
Emerging from what I've once been,
Defeating this battle that has a specific name:
Clinical depression.
Guys, I have become REBORN.

Conflict Attracts Profit

Prelude: *The following poem is an analysis of the continuing conflict that occurs between law enforcement and the black community in America. The killing of unarmed black people at the hands of the police is an act that hits many deep across the nation. This poem references two cases; the murders of Atatiana Jefferson and Botham Jean. In the case of Atatiana Jefferson, her father had placed a restraining order to stop her funeral proceedings. He did so to gain more control of his daughter's funeral arrangements[1]. In the case of Botham Jean, Joshua Brown testified as an eyewitness to Amber Guyger (the cop) murdering Botham in his apartment. A couple days later, Joshua was killed in a parking lot at another apartment complex. Dallas cops have made a couple of arrests in the case, claiming that it was a drug deal gone awry. The cops also claim that the suspected dealers traveled all the way from Louisiana to conduct a drug deal with Joshua. There are some who question those claims, due to the unusual circumstances surrounding his death[2].*

False narrative projected on the befallen,
Turned into a cost-driven end, media not in love with the means.
What's the prize that can be gained from a life?

Complicated regime for the cost of living.
Whose lives matter most?

Schism, fragmentation amongst the Black and the Blue.
Repairable? Where is the root cause?

The media tapping into the distraught emotions
Of the community (the Human Element).

Instant volcano eruption of the Human Element.
But who can fault them?

Suspicions arising about who really did it?!?!?!
Negated trust lost in law enforcement direction,
Clamped by whom; the very few that
Pin the reputation of the righteous many.

Hyper-media creates a daunting narrative:
The Human Element out of control.
Stop the funeral arrangements, I say!!!

For I am no longer in control of my own loss.
Dictated factions through this flash media.
In every social cause, there lies an opportunity for profit.

Grief to those who lost loved ones.
Much is expected of the media, much is given to their higher
influence,
Blatant misuse of the everyday individual builds mistrust.

(And forget about those officers who use their authority for justice
for everyday people.)
For one come all, you shall see
An almost-never-ending carousel of tragedy
That can breed profit and greed.

1. Holcombe, Madeline. "Atatiana Jefferson's father gets a restraining order to delay her funeral and burial". *CNN,* 19 Oct. 2019
2. Shammas, Brittany and Thebault, Reis. "Police name suspects, deny wrongdoing in death of Amber Guyger witness Joshua Brown". *The Washington Post,* 8 Oct. 2019

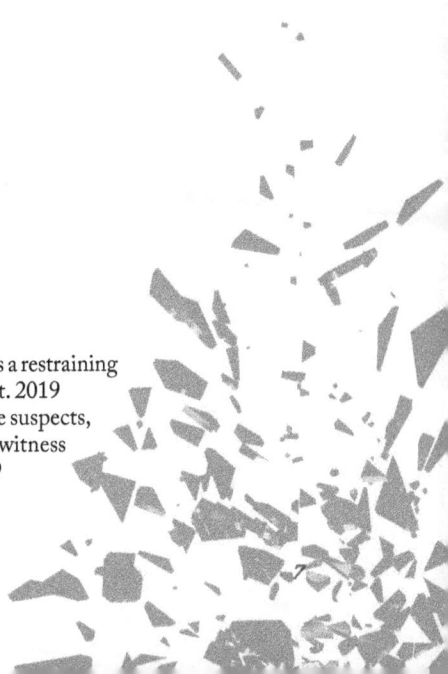

It's Worth Chasing

In it to win it—
Momentum you can feel it,
While blocking your haters' artillery.

A skillset gained—
As you chase your dreams
That does not have an expiration date.

It's going to take discipline,
Infused with infinite patience,
And a community of support.

A crucial factor—
No matter how large or small,
Instilling the belief,
That you can reach those destinations
You so dream about.

The Fear of Failure

My mind is racing;
My thoughts are chasing—
Both distantly
And somehow close by.

Memories that I reflect on
Can leave me in distress—
Tossing and turning at night,
Casting about, asking: what's next?
Or what could have been?

Thoughts that are based in fear
Of what the future has in store for me.
Second-guessing, triple-guessing,
Only got me reminiscing
Of how the scenarios could have potentially been.

But it's when I stop thinking about the outcome,
Start reacting to that gut feeling,
Following my instincts,
And facing up to these challenges in life
That I see their powerful motivation
To becoming the change I want to be.

Becoming more in tune with the infinite—
That's the key to overcoming
The fear of failure.

The World is Yours

Turn on the TV…
Catch the evening news.
What do you see?
Examples and examples and examples of:
Celebrity;
Idolatry;
Tragedy;
Mass shootings—
Anomalies!

Instances of:
Racism;
Inequality;
Systematic oppression;
And bigotry
Leaves one submerged in a sea of paranoia
About their surroundings…
A world where they don't know what to believe.

Which begs the question:
How can one remain unstained in this world?
Answer: By turning off the TV.

When one comes to grips
With the unfairness this world begets
And sees the reality of
The unwavering competition this world fosters
Of one another,
Then one comes to a realization—
That with enough brains, drive, and willpower
One will be able to break through
And succeed over any obstacle—
Beginning to see how
The world is yours.

The Global Reset

Lost in the constellations
Mapping out the world's agenda,
The coronavirus,
Got society
Pushing the panic button.

Life as you know it…
Will not be the same
In the hereinafter.

Markets, the economy,
Adjusting to
A growing digitalized world—
People now embracing,
Running their global businesses
All from a smartphone.

A function of a new reality;
Working from home,
School is back in session,
The conducting of business meetings
With nobody you can see in person—
But can still be in the same room,
Virtually.

The internet and the real world,
Are now interconnected,
Like we've never seen before.

Taking Ownership of Life

It can all feel so surreal:
One minute, you are
Sitting on the couch watching Netflix,
Watching and seeing
How all of life continues to pass you by,
Like looking out the window
Viewing cars come and go
In and out of your periphery.
But in the next note,
As if turning to a new song in life,
Things begin to change.

As some will say, "luck has its way of choosing."
You develop a sense of comfort—
You're in a bigger place, your profile is on the rise.
With infinite patience,
Work ethic, and the power of choice
You start seeing—it was not luck
That brought about this new change.

Rather, self-improvement, sheer resilience,
And showing the universe love and gratitude
For what life has brought you
Has realized a meteoric rise
In your life circumstances.

But, remember this:
Your life is a reflection of all the people you have known
and all whom have known you…
Once you start to think like a winner,
You'll find a way to win.
Thus begins the process
Of the maturation of you.

Exercising the Vernacular

Beyond the limits of conventional wisdom—
Up, up, and away,
Through the seams
Of the scalar skies and vectorized stars,
Reading in between the lines,
Passing through the space-time continuum—
The properties that are deciphered
By your vernacular language
Hold no bounds.
They are at the mercy of the beholder.

With a stroke of genius,
What one can do by playing with the words
At their disposal:
Provide a change in pace, in context,
With the very way words spew out the breath,
Or how one slashes the paper with the pen.

Proving such that,
The power of the vernacular language
Is in the eyes of the beholder
To whom it deems fit.

Decide how to use this power:
Change minds, flip societies,
Turn the world on its axis,
Or shift the perspectives of
You and me.

Mind bending, dimension shifting,
Corralling the most devious of minds
Into a new outlook on life.

Superhero in Our Mind

For many of us, life can be
A continual domino effect of
Trials, tribulations, down and outs—
A forever swinging pendulum
Between peaks and valleys.

You put in all that time in studying,
But didn't get the grade that you wanted.
You put in plenty of energy and ethic at work,
But don't get the praise and recognition you desire.
Seeking—for what can seem like ages—
For what you think you deserve in life,
But finding yourself falling flat on your face with each step.

There's one thing to always remember:
We as humans at our infinite
Are God-like beings.
This continuum of tests in life
Is what proves telling in transmutation.
Improving ourselves, mentally becoming stronger
After overcoming each discord.

With the mind's infinite potential for growth comes
An understanding of this truth:
With your inner divinity,
From once low self-esteem,
Can emerge an optimism of what you can become.

Mentally we can reach a state
That can rival those characters we see in *The Avengers,*
And start to see how we can become
A superhero in our mind.

Something Ain't Right

What a day, what a day—
One of the worst feelings,
Something doesn't feel right.

Your instincts, the intuition;
When the sales pitch sounds good,
Your logical thinking can get too comfortable.

But when your instincts—
Overrides the logic,
The incidental clue
Becomes ever clear.

Distinguishing truth not at the surface,
More often than not
You're being played.

A Public Speaking Soliloquy

People fear most
What they cannot see or control.

An illusion holding you back
From what you do not know.

It's just criminal
How—
Stagnation manipulates you,
To favor the complacent state.

Believe me when I say this.
You too—
Can overcome your biggest fears,
When you face them
Head on.

The fear of public speaking,
Was a fear of mine that—
I was able to hide for many years.
Remaining in the background.
Didn't think my thoughts
Had to be said.

A comfortable state of being,
Not once I saw a problem
That needed to be met.

I remember back at UCF,
Another colleague and I
Were practicing emceeing,
For a banquet that would guest
Old and new members of an organization
We were in.

We practiced, practiced, and practiced,
Had a script that we repeated,
Following a flow to be said.

Now the show has begun,
The attention is on us,
I don't know what happened to me,
There was a disconnect
With my thoughts of the script
And what I actually said.

(Things are not going the way it did at practice)
(Dang, not going as planned, what now?)

Playing it safe
I just did the transitions,
As my colleague did a lot of the heavy lifting
Emceeing...
I did not feel good of my performance at all.

Now, what's the likelihood?
I would be in a position to speak
In front of an audience again

Years later —
Because of encouragement from my old boss
At work,
I joined Toastmasters International,
A non-profit organization
That helps with your public speaking problems.

Needing to get better at quick response to questioning,
I joined,
And from my experiences
It helped me out a lot more.

Toastmasters has helped me realized that,
My fear of public speaking
Was only just an illusion.

Now the skillset of public speaking,
Which was once an afterthought to work on,
Has now become one of my greatest strengths.

The Decider of Art

Art can be conveyed in many forms
From writing, to music, to painting,
To film, to theater, to TV, and even Photoshop.

All can be seen—
judged high
Or low,
Through ceremonies, galas,
And award shows.

Decided on by popular media
As a conduit, a commercial tool
For mainstream propaganda:
Agendas meant to fit amid the confines of the narrative,
Or fall within the trends of the populace.

Factors of influence including, but not limited to:
Race, social class, feminism, and gender fluidity.

But what has seen to be the best judgment of art is…
Due time.

Five years, ten years, fifteen years, and so forth,
What are people still talking about?
Which art is still being sought out?
Classics deemed now,
Back in the day,
Were just another way to get paid.

The fighting for the award, the recognition,
Can be a clout chase
For fame and notoriety.

Always remain appreciative for those
Who enjoy your work,
No matter how large or small.

Because who knows?
Your piece of art may someday
Be seen as a classic in…
Due time.

Bad News Reflection, Part 1

In life, our everyday occurrences
Can become something we get conditioned to;
As is oft said, how do things change, but still remain the same?
But then out of the blue, you hear some news—
Its rarity, its clarity, like getting struck by lightning.

Bad news, piercing the mind,
Permeating it with discourse and pain
Can be hard for the soul to digest.

Looking at one's life—
Young, care-free of the world before you—
With an optimism that can be crushed
By the unexpected.

A reminder of our mortality,
That we all have an expiration date on this Earth.
We can choose to take this
And wither away in nonexistence,
Or take it as a challenge to be our best selves.

What legacy do we want to leave?
What impact do we want to have?
How can we not just live for ourselves,
But live for others?

It is these burning inquiries
That help us figure out
Answers to an age-old question:
What is the meaning of life?

Once these answers are defined,
It can bring clarity to one's mind.

The Perfect Employee

What we continue to find in life
Is what we call "problems"
Will never go away.
You find the solution to one,
And another one will come your way.

We, as humans, will continue to seek to
Solve problems in our everyday lives.
And…
When one has very little trouble and issues in life,
Then one will find distress in the most
Miniscule of obstacles.

And this segues into The Perfect Employee:
One that is very astute, beholden to their role,
Enamored and married to their job.

"Till death do thee part.
The employee seems fit.
The sanctity of marriage to thy work
Is that to which thou commits."

At night, sweating profusely in bed,
Tossing and turning, thinking about
"Did I press send on that email YESTERDAY?!"
Tossing and turning, thinking about
"Did I place the document in the right file cabinet YESTERDAY?!"
Tossing and turning, thinking about
"Did I update that Excel spreadsheet LAST WEEK?!"

With little to feed the employee's yearning
For excitement and adventure outside of work,
This employee seeks it during the working hours.
As the day unfolds —

Drama, negative energy, and a toxic environment
That can start and end with the employee.

But instead, the employee chooses to instigate and prolong
the drama.
In the eyes of the employee
This satisfies the hunger for excitement and
adventure he/she so covets.

I say this…
There is nothing wrong when one loves their job,
Their line of work.
In fact—
when it is not a chore to get up
in the waking hours
And you enjoy what you do—
These are undervalued virtues in today's society.

But I say this…
Please do not forget to feed
Your inner divinity, your soul's yearning,
Do not forget to feed its social well-being,
The curiosity it seeks in finding
Knowledge amongst the world and everyday life.
Enjoy the work you do!

But please…
Do not forget
There are times
You can disconnect from your job.

And I would say,
The life of The Perfect Employee
Is one in which I would not like to engage in.

Tapping into Your Potential

Driving around town
To different parts you've never been,
Surfing the web,
Crossing paths with the newest trends,
Hot cycle topics—
The frivolous headlines that always seem
To catch the corner of your eye.

And you look up,
Seeing the individuals, the "Somebodies,"
Celebs and those most talked about.

You look up:
A world of the lavish, the finer things in life,
What society deems as The Gold Standard,
The shining arc that many wish to cross paths with.

Then thoughts arrive
Deriding those of the less endowed,
Coalescing into feelings of lack.
An envious energy that can manifest as hate—
Not wanting to see another person succeed,
Feelings of glee,
Equivalent to retribution,

Transmute this energy into
Drive, motivation, uplifting yourself
To seek being the best version of you
This is the journey to your mecca.

A Thank You Note
to Your Ancestors

Images of your homeland,
Generations before you who
Immigrated to this new land.

Looking to make new beginnings,
Creating a new rite of passage,
Manifesting a legacy.

For the family, the lineage,
Providing a new lens of life,
A new lease on life,
Its possibilities.

Speaking from the perspective
Of those looking back,
Thankful for the sacrifices,
The pain and suffering
That had to be gone through
To gain a sense of satisfaction.
The results they have brought to you.

And then the beauty of passing down,
The blessings achieved from the work you put in
To the next generations.

Your Definition
(A Double Meaning)

What memories can last
And tend to stick with you.

It was another long day,
Managing the construction project
And finishing a class,
Relating to this industry.

After work,
That I decided—
"Let me check out this wine bar
That I like to go to."

I walk into the spot,
Varying lights,
Scattered and dimming,
Like you are at a late night
Romantic dinner.

Fancy, glossy array of art,
(Nude paintings of women with Darth Vader masks on),
Hang up on the checkered brick walls.

With all the different wines you can imagine,
Throughout the bar.

I take a seat at the counter,
Ordering one of the specials for wine,
Minding my business
Scrolling through my phone
Sipping on the delicious wine.

When this older woman next to me,
Starts a conversation:

"What is your name?"
"What do you do?"

I answered and replied with similar questions;
These are the conventional conversation starters,
For one to get a glimpse into you.

As our discussion progresses,
That I would describe as:
Introspective,
Intellectual,
And enlightening,
She posed this question:

"Owen, what do you want to be when
you grow up?"

At the time I was 25,
And I just started in the construction industry,
I responded:

"I want to be a project manager in construction."

She replied:

"Owen, you are more than just a project manager
in construction."

Now—
Looking back at this memory,
In reflection.

It reminds me not to define myself,
By my job and what I do.

And when it comes to the,
Conventional conversation starters,
The depth of those answers
Can define you.

The Elusive American Dream

Do I feel like writing?
No, not this time,
But unrest troubles the mind.

Sleep
Coming hard to find.
From a glance,
Of the world around you—
It cannot be ignored any longer.

Truth lies,
In between,
These protesting times.

There's a growing dissatisfaction,
Looming at large,
George Floyd's passing has ignited the frustrations from within.

America, the beautiful.
There are many that ask
"Where has that been?"

Wondering back around,
For the search of the American Dream,
One may ask—
Where does their search begin?

A lesson in classism
These invisible boundaries—
Rigid and immoveable,
Like The Great Wall of China.

Locked in
Creating forth,
An unexpected caste system.

This system—
Endangering the aspirations
Of the people at the bottom.
Not realizing—
That admission to the top,
Rising through the boundaries
Are only made for the very few.

Insomnia's Treasure

That feeling, sleeping at night
With the eyes wide open —
Insomnia tends to drift in,
Sifting through the carousel
Of the mind.

Thoughts coming and going
In a blink of an eye,
Capturing what can be
Indescribable in the daytime,
The unattainable —
That feeling.

In the dimness, looking up at the ceiling,
Your mind, bobbing and weaving,
Trying to figure out this moment
In time.
Trying to figure out how this feeling
Can create such turbulence
In the psyche, in the mind.

And then —
A feeling of optimism,
A feeling of newness,
How the world as you know it
Is changing around you.
Can't wander into the past
It's not coming back.

Looking at it from a different frame of mind,
This change is bringing about
A new you
In due time.

Hyperbolic Time Chamber

Everything that we go through in life
Can be bottled up
(Encapsulated in a hyperbolic time chamber)
In a passive state
Of healing and reflection.

Introspective times of enlightenment
That can bring forth
Cracks, holes on the surface of the capsule,
Providing streams,
Outlets for everything
We go through in life.

Relief, a sense of encouragement,
Breathing of new beginnings,
As to set forth,
And to take a step.

Or better yet, break out of the capsule
To paths we once did not believe
Were becoming to us —
Visions and goals that were deemed impossible,
Now feel possible.

With greatness, not for along your horizon,
Achieving clarity might wield
Visions from
An honest assessment of looking at yourself in the mirror.

No matter who and where you are,
There's always room for improvement of one's self.

Removing the blockage of conceit,
Plundering narcissism,
Intercepting the heed from mentors in life—
It's these jewels from others before,
Their mistakes put into practice,
From which you can reach a new level,
As you set foot outside the chamber.

Life is a Game

Do what you gotta do,
So you can do what you want to do.

Game related,
Life that is.

Spinning course,
Body revolving,
Mind evolving,
Never settling for second rate.

A convenient lie
Or doing whatever it will take,
So you can do whatever you want,
In this world.

It wasn't made to give you breaks,
So don't count on it.

The Mask

You know it's like that balance —
Teetering between need and lack.
Forging to be seen, to be heard,
Missing a sense of who you are,
Master of your universe.

The superpower that crushes what life throws at you —
Virtuoso at candid cinematography
Brought to you and directed by none other than
Who else? —
You.

The awards, the accolades, the problems,
And the veil of greed
Are now beneath you.

Results produced from letting go of the ego
that cycles through an endless labyrinth
Of indecisiveness,
A caricature of hesitancy
that always seems to hold you back.

No longer consumed by this ego
Your focus is better.
And patience has laid out its way, its path,
The process.

Hopping on the Flying Nimbus,
Traveling down its way,
Passing through the space-time continuum
Into the forever now in one moment.

Looking back, it was all about yourself:
The one.

Looking at it now,
You exist and the one has become the two,
An outer body experience.
Finding yourself, you find us.

A collaboration that together
Can fulfill a prophecy, a legend,
A history of your lineage, of great men
From their heyday
Empowering a future to uplift the next day.

An experience you cannot put a price on.
Chomping at the bit,
Of the grit with everyday life,
This balance, of the introvert/extrovert,
Seesawing between each side,
Can't seem to find a leveling on this ride.

Teetering back and forth through the game
We call life,
Slowly, but surely unveiling the Mask,
Channeling infinite patience…

Throughout all parts of your life
…And a hustler's ambition to keep going.

It's therapeutic of sorts,
This outer body experience,
Which can be to You…
…And to me.

A Patient Building Block

Sociable, but loner by choice,
It's what the world begets to me,
Changing attitudes to see what's new.

Looking at building friendships; relationships,
But let's slow down the pace
Don't push it.

I'm weary of people who try to force,
A kinship on me.

Coming off fake, a genuine lost interest,
In getting to know one another.

I'm a useful person that is tired of
Feeling used,
Where's my mutual benefits.

My time and attention,
I see it as highly valuable,
I don't just give it to anyone.

The Matrix Transparency

The mind trapped in cognitive dissonance,
An ignorance, at no fault of one's own,
Better now than never,
Slighted by previous teachings of the world
Has become anew.

Chastised, erasing memories
That will always come back—
A painting of life's canvas,
The colors, the textures, thoughts, expressions
Channeling through the stroke of the brush.
A vehicle, providing an outlet to your mind,
Broadening the mind, pushing the limits
Of your mental capacity.

Your destiny can be found
By following your premonition—
Powerful guidance by one's inner divinity.

If all else fails,
Revert back to your original premise:
A visualization that
The answers to life are inside you.

Patience, the changing of mindset,
Habits transforming, transposing what
Stoicism can gift to you.

A stairway to a new self,
Propelling you to new heights.
That was once upon a time
Seen as nonexistent.

The world seems to have counted you out
Time and time again,
But the continued reinvention,
The mastering of self,
Has unleashed the supernatural.

An individual that has found themselves.
Aligned with the uniqueness of the human genotype,
Teleporting yourself through different realms
Of hidden knowledge.

Making the most unknown, known
For you, seeing the world for what it is,
And navigating it as such.

The Gathering

How many years?
It's been so long since your presence
Has been gifted by family.

A longing to be seen, not forgotten.
Reaching back to the roots
From where it all began,
Stories told through the perspective
Of elders, remembrance of your younger days.

Soaked in smile and laughter,
An energy that cannot be put into words
Has taken over you.
Throwing your neurotransmitters
All out of sorts,
Realigning your body's internal wiring,
Manifesting an aura, a glow,
That walks with you
Everywhere you go.

No amount of time, distance, or misunderstanding
Can sever the bond of family.

The Duality Mindset

The continued spinning,
The forever rotation
Lathered by an endless flow of energy
Powering the curiosity—
It's how the mind works.

The aspect of finding what's new,
Taking on new challenges, driving the mind
To learn to overcome different obstacles—
That's multi-tasking, multi-level managing,

Lead by example, by your comfort
In cruise control of everlasting life,
Presents a powerful you
Not easily perturbed by nonsense.

Detail oriented—
Certain little things
That caused distress in the past
Are now just a blip on the radar.

Life has begun to slow down;
Everything in front of you now seems to be
Captured in focus.

You were raised to become
A thinking individual who
Develops the Duality Mindset:
The combination of left-brain and right-brain thinking.
No longer polarized by one-sided thinking.

This new way of looking at life, produces
One:
The power of understanding
Reconciling opposites,
And embracing a natural thing in life —
Duality.

Comprehending what encompasses all.
The differences in people,
Taking a step back
To look at things from new angles.

Continuing to seek perspectives;
Messages cannot be received if the mind is not open.
Defeating the nature of greed and temptations
To not alter decision-making, your perspective.

Bias will always travel parallel with the perspective,
But seeing from different vantage points
Can better explain the why and the how in
What others do and think.

No longer following blindly,
A yearning for an answer in the Revelations, of when
Bypassing the messiah complex,
The false divine intervention.

In doing so,
An activation of the mind over mind is achieved,
And becoming your own you.

And You Didn't?

Ohh…
So you changed now.

A constant variable in life.

A meaningful change,
So you can start owning you,
And not let the world run you.

The Winners' Circle

Touché, as promised,
That ray of hope: gliding, rotating,
Skipping through the different factions of the spectrum,
Like a crystal ball of sorts, beaming
An array of colors to different aisles of the sector.

This new feeling, this new energy—
Orbiting, revolving,
A radiating transparency,
Breaking through the walls that guards
One's inner self: "The Knowing."

An inspiration, time being spent
Space traveling to various corners, galaxies
Your mind has not seen or ventured to—
A new belonging,
Like-minded cohorts, where
The genius is crafted and molded.

The natural you is resonating,
Unlocking another portal,
Impacting others' lives too
That bears fruits
With the rewards of the fortunate.

Boomerang, coming back to you,
A selfless embracement on THE WHY
You do the things you do.
You want to see others succeed.
The helping hand equating goals for
You and I to achieve.
Raising the bar to new heights
That once started out as a dream.

Taking advantage of kindness for weakness
Can present attitudes clouding judgment,
Blocking you from going on in life.

Arriving at a new circle, galaxy,
Leaving impressions, which make you wonder—
Groundbreaking, mind shattering—
How mindset changes when you're within
A different circle.

The connections sparking,
No more dodging,
A deeper look into your past,
An examination providing a window,
A deeper look into your future.

On the opposite side of all crises
There lies an opportunity:
"The Showing," a reminder that life
Can and will present better times.

No more backseat driving of life.
You're captaining your own ship,
Championing grace merits,
Crown seeking, leveling up.

A belief the virtuous one
Is not leading astray, but…
Opening new avenues.

Everything in life happens for a reason—
An understanding patience, growth,
A "once upon a time," was not ready.

Preparation meeting opportunity,
Equalizing the moments.
Intention's force field amongst the universe
Is neither created nor destroyed,
But transferred to new spirits—
Captivating a new generation of life's worth
To the masses.

Bouncing Back

Face clapped between sweaty palms,
An uneasiness clenching you through and through.
At the tip of your mind, the sub-psyche is placed into orbit:
A consciousness reaching levels.

You don't know where you are,
How you got here,
A disregard of your surroundings.
(Subconsciously, you don't care
Because life has won this battle.)

Distraught—
Glued to the chair, the bed,
You think things are going to change on their own,
Like good luck is supposed to come your way,
By chance.
Ask yourself... Why?

Why do you think the things you want in life are to come easy?
An infinite loop,
Doing the same things, expecting different results.
It will never change.

The defeatist attitude is attained when
The outcome does not equate the predicted results.
When your ego is directing your life—
Forcing moves that timing does not call for,
Rushing into mistake after mistake—
It leads to frustrations of the uncontrollable.

Let go, switch course away
From the ego, and let the mind roam free,
Moving on from the defeatist attitude.

And changing your thoughts
Will change how you view life—
Gaining a new attitude, a confidence.

The mind is at ease again.

Bouncing back, don't let up,
And seize the day…

Controlling the Motive

Motionless, fragmented, like the shattering of glass,
Putting this spell on your mind.

It's the long game—
One's desires non-existent at the surface,
Cloaked and wrapped underneath.
It's the different signs, the non-verbal cues.

It is what's not shown that holds the answers
To questions that are not asked outright.
A trailblazer,
memories begin to rewind from your mind—
The shattered glass pieces start to look like a puzzle.

Contrite at naivety, now navigating exquisitely,
Seeing the answers before the questions surface.
Experience really is the best teacher
And the tutelage of mentorship.

Grasping another look at human behavior,
An analysis from the unwelcome study of the relationship —
A game indeed, a business,
One that can teleport one's life situation
To an out-worldly portal.

Strife, greed, the painting of a façade,
Back-turning, revenge-seeking, backstabbing:
Things weren't always what they seemed to be.

Chills rumbling down your spine.
Stop keeping score—
It's that perception of what's mine is mine,
What's yours is yours,
That is actually slowing the growth of people.

This angst that tends to ride among us —
Wanting to outdo your fellow associates,
Forgetting the significance of giving
But not expecting.

Don't play yourself because there is that balance,
That line drawn in the sand
Between giving and being used.

Life lessons have painted that line in the sand, oh, so clearly!
Selflessness is a must, but the character
Of one's being — it needs to be assessed
And established.

As an individual, your agenda has to be put in place,
Learning how to play the game
In all parts of your life.

A must — sticking to this agenda, unequivocally,
No bending at the will for the fruits of others,
But dealing among those, in tune with your agenda —
Creates an opening to a growing you.

Physically and mentally, at near-optimal proficiency,
Morphing into a gladiator,
The palm reads a telepathic alliance.

This gladiator,
Walking through life with unyielding dominance,
Conquering the challenges that life throws at you,
Feelings of jealousy and retribution melting away,
And finding a way to win.

Discovering this voice in you
Guiding you through and through.
Nothing can get in the way.
Of what you was destined to do.

Stability Shifting

Planning your escape,
Of where?
The forever going nowhere.

Mind numb to the world's worries,
A cold atmospheric ambience,
Grasp the heart's desires,
In tune with the following of your own thinking
Trapped by clues,
Human behavior of familiar faces.

A beginning of thoughts,
To seek new pastures
Where new location is determined by potential growth.

A changing of priorities,
At forth, now looking to where this potential,
Can turn into much more.

When the Beta Becomes an Alpha

My, my, the sabbatical
Crescendo involvement of self
In tune to the sparse understandings of one's surroundings.

The beta becoming an alpha—
Resounding interlude,
Crashed insignificance of the prior.

Applied knowledge of others onto you.
Remixed, a gravitas of how people see you,
Old behavior 'tis thwarted.

A condition that required
A mental purge, mind metamorphosis,
Time will gift what instincts have prophesied:
Soul transfiguration, body alteration in crescendo.

How the mastering of what can be controlled
You...
Can inflict on your environment
Expensive taste, high standards—
You only want the best of the best.

Because that's how you see yourself—
Of steep value, entrenched,
Seeping in the veins,
Cold-blooded, bold, self-assured.
An aggressive showing now pronounced
Nature has knighted upon you.

It's the developing of new leaders,
Boy becomes man,
A proceeding that cannot be shortcut.
Complacency will only rewind.

The growth, embracement of the spiral theory.
At any moment in man's life,
One is either spiraling upward or downward,
A complacent state equates downward mobility.

Going in circles of sorts,
From one's year-to-year analysis,
Tactical insertion —
Look on how one can re-define
Their future in their own hands.

What everybody likes is of no consequence.
Distractions are muted,
Nullifying disrespect to the tune of
Blissful ignorance.

Bringing peace to a wistful calling,
Only dealings amongst those that add to one's peace.

It's a clarity.

Uncluttering of the mind,
How this calling breathes new life and vision in man.
Civil liberties truncate a life of servitude.
It's your dream you want to be working toward,

It's your dream that you ought to grind for.
A finding of yourself in disparaging accords
With society's constructed timeline of the working people.

At new frequencies immersed with the universe,
With efforts in production,
Of getting out the rat race:
The minus of selfish desires.

An orientated outlook of how you can
Impact and bring change to people's lives

By also improving yourself,
Which will resonate onto others too.

Not leaving this Earth without attempting your life's passion(s).
Your inner divinity's true worth,
Regardless of the results of one's efforts.

A growing satisfaction will linger into old age,
Of the knowing that efforts were partaking
To live out your dreams,
And not somebody else's.

Bad News Reflection, Part 2 (Yepez)

Why Him?
Unbeknownst to life's becomings,
Weeps of the rain droplets,
Falling from the storm,
Cancerous to the mind's thoughts.

Begrudging the unexpected: can't take it in.
Do not want to believe this is happening.
He was a good guy, not a troublemaker,
Loved by those in the know of him,
The man within.

Faltering loosely, the conscious clinging
To the good times, the memories
That will always live forever.

Pain dissolving, sending condolences,
This one hits you tough — disbelief.
A mirror introspective,
Looking at yourself, seeking clarity,
No different from any other man.

Transcending your ego, you look now at
Life beyond yourself — a reminder of your mortality.
People are in your life for seasons, reasons, or a lifetime.

As such,
No matter what happens, regardless of circumstances,
They will never go away —
Life is too valuable.

Reincarnated, life after death,
A legacy remembered by those close.
Leaving a piece of you amongst
Those in the three-dimensional world.

Gone too soon.
I ask again to the Lord, The Higher Power that be,
"Why him?!?!?!"

A slight lapse in reason, fumigating emotion,
Tepid at its core of the understanding.
Your inner divinity arises from the human body
To see light in a new beginning.

Becoming more in tune with the Universe,
Your spirit permeates among us, resting easy our souls,
Our hearts vivid.

A new day in passing, halting cynically rooted thoughts.
Refreshed, the mind can grow from this turbulence,
An ending that will spark many to see the world,
With a new lens—perception.

Let live a new day and
Rest easy, my friend…

The Blueprint

Your destiny—
A fallacy when put in others' hands.
Riding in the passenger seat of life,
Stopping and going, drifting, hitching off-rail.

The vehicle of life—your life—is careening
                Out of control,
      Your control.

But the fault belongs to whom?
The person in the mirror.
How can you arrive at your life's destination
When you're not even in the driver's seat?

Take back control, hands on the steering wheel,
Switching lanes,
Finding the path that defines you.

Once in that lane, hit the gas pedal—accelerate.
Now you're on the highway of your life,
The environment bending at your will,
Conforming to your reality.

Now on a mission—
Purpose has discovered you.

At first it can seem a daunting task
To gain full control of your life.

What you are exposed to
Can determine what you think is
Possible or not

The television cohorts,
Sprouting a life to many — a fantasy.
A celebrity's reality will look to be of
A different world,
Screwing up the mind's chassis like Frankenstein.

The Walking Dead
Comfortability, the selling of dreams —
That's nature's concocted ingredients for
The recipe of the followers.

Many minds are fiends for a taste
Of the celebrities' reality — the drug —
The instant gratifications can be addictive.
My money gets jealous.

Finding your gift(s) in life can be of
Such delay,
Hastily making you want something new and exciting to fall
in your lap.
But one with a purpose, one that has found their gift(s)
That he/she works to master —
A combination of looks, charisma, sense of oneself, and uniqueness —
Stands out from the rest.

Outkast[3] in the world of the many.
Just seeming to be in your own reality.
Finding the conduit to use one's gift(s)
To serve and help people's lives.

The measurement of the people impacted
Will beget the metaphysical of attracting money:

The Blueprint

Be an engineer of your craft
Shining in the lives of many.

[3.] Outkast is the name of an American hip-hop group
originating from Atlanta, Georgia

Corporate America

It's the lion in you—
The aggression,
A force within you made by nature that
Cannot be tamed or domesticated.

Eruptions occur at ill-fated times—
Unexpected guilt trips, stubbornness
That others can find difficult to deal with.

The domesticated arena around you
In tolerance of you,
The force within you can only go on so forth.

Meeting the day-by-day, week-by-week orders
To be in compliance with others.
Serving another's dreams separate from yourself.
What's the reward for being an employee?

Corporate America;
An arena built tough for many, but not everybody.
Rooted in everyday facades,
Everything's out in the open only when you're not around.

The same old vacations,
Repeated in rotation year 'round,
A glimpse of your happiness subsiding,
Kiss ass before you can kick it.
Tailor made for an environment of backstabbing.

Save yourself, let thy brother drown.

After a year, a continuum monotonous overture of tasks,
Over and over and over again,
Sailing through sullen quarters.

But then, this arena is a haven for many,
Providing financial support to enjoy life as available to them.
Work environment run by strict-but-understanding and sometimes-
lenient leadership
Can be endured.

Work in an arena with people/cliques that you like—
Friendships built outside of work that let you
Laugh, have good times while working,
Smiles and get-togethers.

Sure, there will be pitfalls.
Of course co-workers are going to talk behind each other's backs…
…That's human nature.

But when the corporate arena can feel like a family unit,
This is not just a company you work for.
This is a team, working together in unison to accomplish the
tasks at hand,
And conquering problems as they announce themselves.

Upper management in allowance of paid time off,
With accommodating accord,
Few pushbacks,
Albeit with proper notice,
Can make Corporate America not feel like a chore
For the everyday individual.

How About That

One person changed,
One person impacted,

By your service(s).

Is one more than,
How the world would have stayed,

By you remaining complacent.

Do You Believe?

A master of your own kingdom,
Beauty, crass maneuvering,
Nature unraveling its layers time and again—
That's the craft of writing.

Science ought to be tribute-d.
A Higher Power faith be in
A dichotomy that can seem to find no balance—
The abstract, a gold mine of information.

You will never run out of material to write about.
For yourself, it's a never-ending manhunt for something,
Anything new to write about—
A new epiphany, a new inspiration,
And so on, and so on.

Manifestations of new writings again and again,
Remarkable in their stark contrast of knowing.
This poem was written on a whim, out of the blue,
Freestyling each line as it goes from what is unknown to true.

How do I do this? I don't know.
The only thing that grows in life naturally is you.
But this skillset of poetry writing, freestyling,
Has developed in such a state that it has become
Natural.

When I started this poem,
I did not know what to write about.
I just went, and as I wrote,
My thoughts in unison with the pen and the pad,
A trichotomy found a balance
In a cluttered mind.
Writing continues to be an outlet for clearing my mind.

Through these poetic lines,
One can get a glimpse into me,
A conventional avenue for expressing myself,
That was once a path I would not have believed.

Diamonds are forever.
Jettison details, nuances, crafted in a number of ways,
Your ways, engineering your craft as it seems fit.
Have optimal credence in you and your talents.

I will continue to write 'till I am no longer.
But my writing is like diamonds—
I will continue to exist forever through these lines,
Lines hitting the reader like the devil's candy,
A dose of braggadocios.

To self: an indoctrinated dogma,
Alleviating qualms.

If one does not feel such about their craft and what they do,
Then who will?

Observation of The Moment

A look at the picture can take your breath away:
Glean sciences en route pursuant to life's answers,
An overt reasoning on everything
In time can be explained.

The nuances flip the reasoning—
"This can't be, it's not making sense,"
A left-brain, linear way of thinking.

Illogical revelation.
It doesn't add up,
The complexity of people, the mind, and life's worth
Cannot be quantified, dissected rationally.

The manipulation of numbers and studies
Will not define the non-biological—
Human nature.

Distortion of numbers and studies
Benefits the invested creed:
"Survival of the fittest,"
An evolution of one to their environment.

How life experiences interact,
A day-to-day study,
A better understanding of oneself,
Separating the watched and the watcher.

Scientific studies have no answers to these moments
That are both in and out of control of oneself.

Manipulating human emotions—
Watch you lose your calm,
Triggering the outburst,
Hitting a nerve—
Unexpected reactions to outside influences
That are not "deemed fit."
"Insanity" is the proclamation.

It's how the outside supremacy
Can control the individual:
Puppet string master,
mastering through the promise of reward
Set forth, out of reach of the individual.
Breaking one to follow a new goal,
A new agenda
Controlling his/her motives.

Observe the moment:
There are those that
By watching others' behavior
Use a level of rationality to control people
And what can be an instance in your life circumstances
Can affect your livelihood,
Your course for an indefinite period of time...

Facade's Clone

The way I see it—
Sight, life's scope,
Seen through the mirrored prism,
A kaleidoscope of colors reflecting time's nuisance.

The procrastination,
What are you waiting for?
What do you really want to be doing?
What's holding you back from pursuing your dreams, your goals?

A cozy fraudulence envelopes you
When coasting through
Another person's vision,

The facade that can be seen through
The mirrored prism,
A front—
This isn't you.

Outside influences reveal the façade.
Lost genuineness passed over by revelations,
Moments relegated to forgotten reminders
Of what your calling in life is.

Full speed ahead as these signs.

You watch and see it pass again and again;
It's what brings a smile to your face.
No façade,
A radiation of your true colors amongst the spectrum.

'Tis life gracious thee,
When thou find what makes life so gracious.

An ambivalent abundance mindset
Got you overthinking the results.

Do what makes you happy.
The results will come afterward.
The clock's ticking for you to end your façade.
The question is: Are you going to end it…?

Commentary on Selected Poems

BAD NEWS REFLECTION, PART 2 (YEPEZ)

This poem was inspired by the passing in September 2019 of Adam Yepez, a good friend and colleague of mine from the University of Central Florida (UCF).

One morning, I received a call from another friend and colleague of mine, Johnny. On one of his social media feeds, he saw posts that Adam had passed. I didn't want to believe it. I checked my feed and saw the posts for myself. I called his number and texted him, with no response. Then I got in contact with one of Adam's hometown friends and she confirmed he had passed from a very rare form of cancer, sarcoma cancer.

At work that morning, it wasn't easy to console myself and be productive. One of my favorite outlets is writing, so I composed this poem while at work.

Johnny, Adam, and I graduated together with bachelor's degrees in civil engineering. UCF's nickname is "You Can't Finish," and it was a difficult journey. If it weren't for those guys, I wouldn't have graduated. We each played a part in seeing one another succeed and finish. I called the poem "Yepez" because that's what Adam's friends called him back in his hometown.

THE BLUEPRINT

When hip-hop group, Outkast, came to early prominence in 1994, southern US hip-hop acts were not as respected as their eastern and western peers in mainstream hip-hop.

At the 1995 Source Hip-Hop Music Awards, Outkast received the award for "Best New Hip-Hop Group." Upon receiving the award, Outkast was met with boos. In his acceptance speech, Andre 3000 said, "The South got something to say, that's all I got to say."

Outkast went on to have one of the greatest careers in music with a discography that, in my opinion, very few hip-hop artists rival.

In sharing this bit of hip-hop history, I want to drive home this point. Many people I've met who have experienced considerable financial success have told me that they gained their success by examining what the masses are doing, then doing the opposite. More often than not, when you pursue your dreams, you will become an "Outkast" in your regular social circles.

CORPORATE AMERICA

LINES OF INSPIRATION (REFERENCES)

"Save yourself, let thy brother drown."

This is a quote from one of my co-workers at JCB Construction, Clem Seegobin.

DISCUSSION

He told me this after a situation at work where I was at fault, but only because I was busy trying to get a task completed for somebody else. More specifically, I was helping out the general contractor we were working under.

Finger-pointing can be a common occurrence while working in corporate America. In the beginning, when I was "green"—just starting out—I would go out of my way to help others and solve their problems. In essence, I was expending my energy and time in completing other people's tasks instead of my own. I was unfocused and ineffective at work. What seemed to be productive to the project team to an inexperienced eye—my own—was actually unproductive.

The corporate controller at JCB Construction, Priscilla Robinson, told me I needed to concentrate on the requirements of my position. Since then, and after incorporating Clem's quote, navigating the construction management field has become easier.

Prelude to My Grandpa's Eulogy

In the last week of June 2019, my mother and I traveled to Jamaica to attend the funeral of my late grandfather, Theophilus Altimond Greenwood, who had died in May 2019 at the age of ninety-four. Not only was it a tough loss for the family, but also it was my first-time visiting Jamaica in nine years. I will admit to some nervousness, especially when my mother told me that I would be giving the eulogy. I felt immense pressure to do it right.

When I first arrived, seeing my loved ones in Jamaica again was indescribable. It was a feeling that, honestly, I hadn't felt in a long time. There was warmth, genuine welcome, and love in seeing each other again. What I like most about visiting my family in Jamaica is how the lifestyle is night and day from here in the States. My grandparents live in the Jamaican rural countryside. On my mom's side, they live in the Alps in Cockpit Country's parish, Trelawny. On my dad's side, his family lives near the parish Portland. These areas are not as urbanized as the States, and the lifestyle is more laid-back and easygoing.

The funeral was on June 30, 2019, which is the same day as my dad's birthday. He traveled to Jamaica for the funeral that weekend. During the period prior to the funeral, I interviewed my relatives about Grandpa and composed the eulogy based on their answers. I gave that speech in in the church in front of a crowd of at least 60, maybe 100 people. It was nerve-wracking at first, but I was able to settle in.

Later, I received positive responses from the funeral attendees about it. While it sure was a lot different from giving speeches in Toastmasters' club meetings in front of five to seven people, those meetings prepared me to give the eulogy in Jamaica.

Below is the eulogy I wrote for my grandfather.

Grandpa's Eulogy

In loving memory and dedication to the memory of
Theophilus Altimond Greenwood.

"Good afternoon everyone. For those who do not know who I am, my name is Owen Bryan Jr., also known as David by loved ones. I am from foreign (lands). I am the grandson of the deceased, Theophilus Altimond Greenwood. I want to extend appreciation to family, friends, and loved ones for coming out on this blessed day to honor the loss of a great man. An amazing great-grandfather, grandfather, father, uncle, brother, husband, and brethren, Mr. Altimond Greenwood was born in the year of 1924 on this beautiful island of Jamaica. In his day, Mr. Altimond grew up to be a splendid farmer, and a devoted Christian and Seventh Day Adventist, along with his lovely dear wife, Aldith Greenwood, my grandmother. Both Altimond and Aldith ended up being great strongholds in the Alps, always willing to serve the church and their community. Their marriage lasted an amazing 66 years. Their union bore five children, ten grandchildren, and three great grandchildren.

"Remembrance can be of good times. And the Alps, or wherever how far, will see Mr. Greenwood as a high-character, strong willed man. A man of few words, Altimond was also a funny man. One of my favorite stories my grandma would share was when I was little, grandpa would put me up on a donkey and show me how to ride it. I would always get excited when he did this for me. One thing I remember about Grandpa was every time you greeted him; he always gave a big smile that could brighten up anyone's day. I will leave you with this quote from Altimond: "Anything you do, you do to yourself." This is about karma—if you do good in life, good will come back to you. As I leave you with these words of his, I want to thank Grandpa for the legacy he has left for us. He may be gone from this Earth, but he forever live in our memories…"

www.ingramcontent.com/pod-product-compliance
Lightning Source LLC
LaVergne TN
LVHW041234080426
835508LV00011B/1210